# Green Green Grass :
# A Poetic Auto Bio

Chelsea Riley

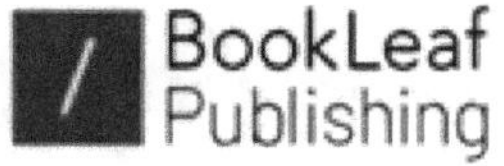

Presentation by *BookLeaf Publishing*

Web: www.bookleafpub.com

E-mail: info@bookleafpub.com

ISBN: 9789357213448

First edition 2023

# The Bio

Chelsea
Petite, Tender, Tricky, Audacious.
Daughter of Bruce and Holly
Loves Art, Nature, Mr. Riley.
Feels passionate, exposed, overwrought.
Needs shelter, nourishment, love.
Gives love, generosity, time.
Fears war, anger, the unknown.
Wishes for peace, assurance, a stiff drink.
Lives in the crossroads of America
Riley

# To Bruce

2

It's Christmas time:
A smile on paper is a memory in gold.
When I'm in your arms, I'm the tallest around.
I long for more memories than tales, having
drowned.

It's Late November:
The bitter cold is brisk in the air,
And always heavy on my heart.
It was far too soon for our journey to part.

# To Holly

3

My first role model.
All knowledge of womanhood,
I got it from you.

# Art

How independently
She took her step
Of Enhanced design.

~To Audrey

# Nature

Green, green grass; The secrets you hide,
With all your wildlife that resides deep inside.
From feral young creatures that bounce through shrubs,
To time telling crickets, and hoppers and grubs.

Green, green grass; What a comfort you bring,
Like the perfection made by a picnic in spring.
Hold our blanket please, and I'll open the wine.
Pairs well with sunlight, and your invite to dine.

Green Green Grass; we see your strength.
Look beyond modest efforts, no matter what length.
Walked on each day, yet you remain with each tread -
Ice will dry from your back, and you rise from the dead.

Green Green Grass; I'd know you anywhere.
Driving state line to the next, or from a plane in the air.
Oh but the day I crossed the ocean - to sing as a joyful lass -

I saw your emerald beauty; your radiance and glow; your green, green grass.

# Mr. Riley

If I asked for love, would it even hold true?
If I asked for happiness,
Would it cause me to feel blue?

The mystery lingered through parts of my life
Like the brightness of red
With a cut from a knife.

Oh, but the answers given to me
Were more than my aspirations,
Because the truth is...

It's not only love:
It's warmth.
It's comfort.
It's cherished.
It's you.

It's not only happiness:
It's laughter,
It's eager,
It's adventure,
With you.

So when what I longed for
Was True Love's Happiness,
All along standing there -
Was you.


<3 For Kris.

# Passionate

9

I dream of a world where
A dream for a girl
Is not an aspiration,
But a realization for a woman,
And an inspiration for our children's children.

#empoweredwoman

Dedicated to Joan Ruth Bader Ginsburg

# Exposed

The art of bare flesh
Entwined with sparkles and chords.
Take your bow, Gorgeous.

~Dedicated to the Drop Dead Darlings
Burlesque and Variety Troupe

# Overwrought

I can't sleep tonight - close not one eye.
The beauty has fallen from the sky.
Now it's ash beneath my feet
Burning in the raging heat.

What a blow -
So forceful and raw,
Which can leave you dripping
Like the winter's first thaw.

The whispers I hear are soft on my skin
Like velvet and silk, sweetly swaddling me in.
But the cloak becomes heavy - not wrappings,
but ties.
Can I ever escape these curdling cries?

No sleep again last night -
I just lied in bed
With thoughts and convictions
Whirling deep in my head.

The break of dawn demands so much.
I rush to my vices to stay in touch.
Wash my face, and swallow a pill.
Wash down the screams, evermore so shrill.

How did the day become so distraught?
With paradoxical laughter, I become
overwrought.
Overcome with the screams and the rage,
My heart has suddenly stolen the stage.

So take me home and lie with me.
The battle is far too strong to fight singly.
Help me bury the pressure down deep,
Or just hold me tonight - and allow me to sleep.

# Shelter

In a bitter snow,
It's warmth.

In suffocating heat,
It's fresh air.

In times of extraneous chaos,
It's protection.

When I'm surrounded, but desperately alone.
It's what my soul hungers.
It's time to go home.

# Nourishment

Decadent and creamy macaroni and cheese:
The Italian plate that will always appease.
I'm not quite full
So I'll hold out my bowl,
And politely exclaim "More Please!"

A savory casserole made with green beans:
The finest of American comfort cuisines.
A creative way
To truthfully say,
"Yes, Mother, I ate all my greens."

Pork Chop...
Chops of um...?
Oh My...they are...

...

...

Yum!

# Love

Can you hear a rhythm
Without a beat?
Like treading the desert
Without sand in your feet?

To take away love
Can take away breath -
You can take my heart
And trade it for death.

I don't need to see you,
I just need your touch.
But not to feel you
Can lose sight of so much.

To lose sight of
What's all around,
Becoming lost
To never be found,

If no one loves me
No one will find me.
So what will become
Of my lost sense to be?

# Generosity

Just like a hydrant
Just off the street,
Let me pour over
Your fury and heat.

Envision me
As a waterfall.
Flowing energy
With which I enthrall.

To take a sip
Is, of course, no trouble.
But a droughting cliffside
May leave me to rubble.

It wasn't your fault
To want but a drink,
But I reached too far,
Plunging over the brink.

Lost in a free fall,
I'm out of control.
Plummeted down,
I face my toll.

Now I'm parched
With nothing to share
But single raindrops
After storms in the air.

It's hard to find me -
I'm now remnants of the flood.
Yet you still call my name
As you walk through the mud.

# Time

So much more than
The ticking of clocks
But a gift wrapped in bows
'Round a decorative box.

A present that's mine,
The presence in time,
To know where to find you
With a gentle chime.

There must be reason
To sit and wait.
Something must come too soon
To cause being too late.

For the world to impart
We give and take as we choose
What is no one's to own,
But everyone's to lose.

# War

Why go down in blazing glory
When the battle is but part of the story?

When hatred can linger for so many years,
Our faces are stained with permanent tears.

Lady Liberty gazes from far and up high,
While inside she sobs her gentle cry.

# Anger

Tell me to "Calm down,"
I promise;
It gets worse from there.


Dedicated to all the angry women - Do Not
Calm Down!

# Unknown

With petals made of shattered glass,
A stem that's crowded in thorns;
Roots that hang like single threads,
This sprouted seed that mourns.

~~~

To walk this barbed garden
Where poison waits to bite,
The only armor that can be worn
Is lack of doubt or fright.

~~~

Pour over me, sweet moisture,
And soak me with your bliss.
Mend my skin to woven silk
Soft as a petals kiss.

~~~

For if I never smell again
Or see the light of day,
Anyone can walk the garden
And become it's prey.

~~~

But instead
Let's water it
Let's cherish it

~~~

And have a beautiful bouquet.
~~~

# Peace

It's a nice, warm day;
So I'll lie in the hammock
And peacefully sway.
The breeze can ease the sorrow
Of tales told by tomorrow.

# Assurance

Do you know me?
Do you see my face?
Sitting beside you
In this place?
Do you notice me
Do you hear my voice?
Do you know my opinion
Of any choice?
Do you think of me
When you breathe the air?
Do you take a moment
To even care?
Do you feel the hunger
That I starve inside?
Starving for Love,
And Beauty, and Pride.
Do you understand me?
Do you feel my pain?
Piercing my heart,
And screaming in vein?
Did you know I'm a person
Just like you?
I bleed, I break,
And I have feelings too.
Did you ever meet me?

Or shake my hand?
Or did you just simply judge,
Without trying to understand?
Do you know if you take time
To get to know me,
We might have things in common,
Just wait and see.
Remember next time
When you see me walk by;
Bright my day
And take the chance to say hi.
Did you know that all
You had to say?
Maybe even to help me
Live just one more day?


~Featuring the Younger Chelsea
~ Don't worry, Kiddo. It only gets better.

# A Stiff Drink

25

Drink to better well being.
Down the things we neglected everyday.

Drink so the drink
Bears the reality
In any other form.

It's that essential.

# The Crossroads of America

26

In the heart of the crossings
No story too old;
Desires from the blue and gold.
Indy cars racing,
All the tulips encasing.
Never once said goodbye to
A sugar cream pie.

www.ingramcontent.com/pod-product-compliance
Lightning Source LLC
LaVergne TN
LVHW050247200726

843509LV00015B/2927